Stitching the Night Away 2019 Cross Stitch and Blackwork Sampler

Loretta Oliver

Stitching the Night Away

I would like to take a moment to thank you for purchasing this pattern booklet. **I truly appreciate your support.**

Please visit **www.StitchingtheNightAway.com** to leave a comment or send me a photo of your finished projects to add to the gallery. I love seeing what people create with these patterns! It's beautiful to see how we can all start with the same pattern and come out with such unique finished projects.

CONTENTS

ABOUT THE PATTERN

The pattern size is 161 wide by 213 height in stitches.

You'll find that the pattern is without a floss legend or color key. That is done intentionally, the idea here is to customize your own piece to your liking, using whatever floss colors you feel most drawn to at the time. This is your project and I want you to enjoy the process and come away with a piece that is as unique as you are.

The blackwork is shown on the pattern as red lines, but this is only to make it easier to read against the black grid lines. It's also worth noting here that this type of decorative blackwork is really just backstitching in disguise, no fancy technique required.

I've set the layout up to have patterns on one side of the paper throughout the booklet so that if you wish to mark things inside the book you'll have the space to do so and also to make scanning and copying out "working copies" a little bit easier to do for those that prefer not to mark their original copies.

Have fun and happy stitching!

FULL PATTERN SINGLE PAGE

LARGE PRINT PATTERN – PART 1 (TOP LEFT)

LARGE PRINT PATTERN – PART 2 (TOP RIGHT)

LARGE PRINT PATTERN – PART 3 (BOTTOM LEFT)

LARGE PRINT PATTERN – PART 4 (BOTTOM RIGHT)

INDIVIDUAL BLOCKS – 1

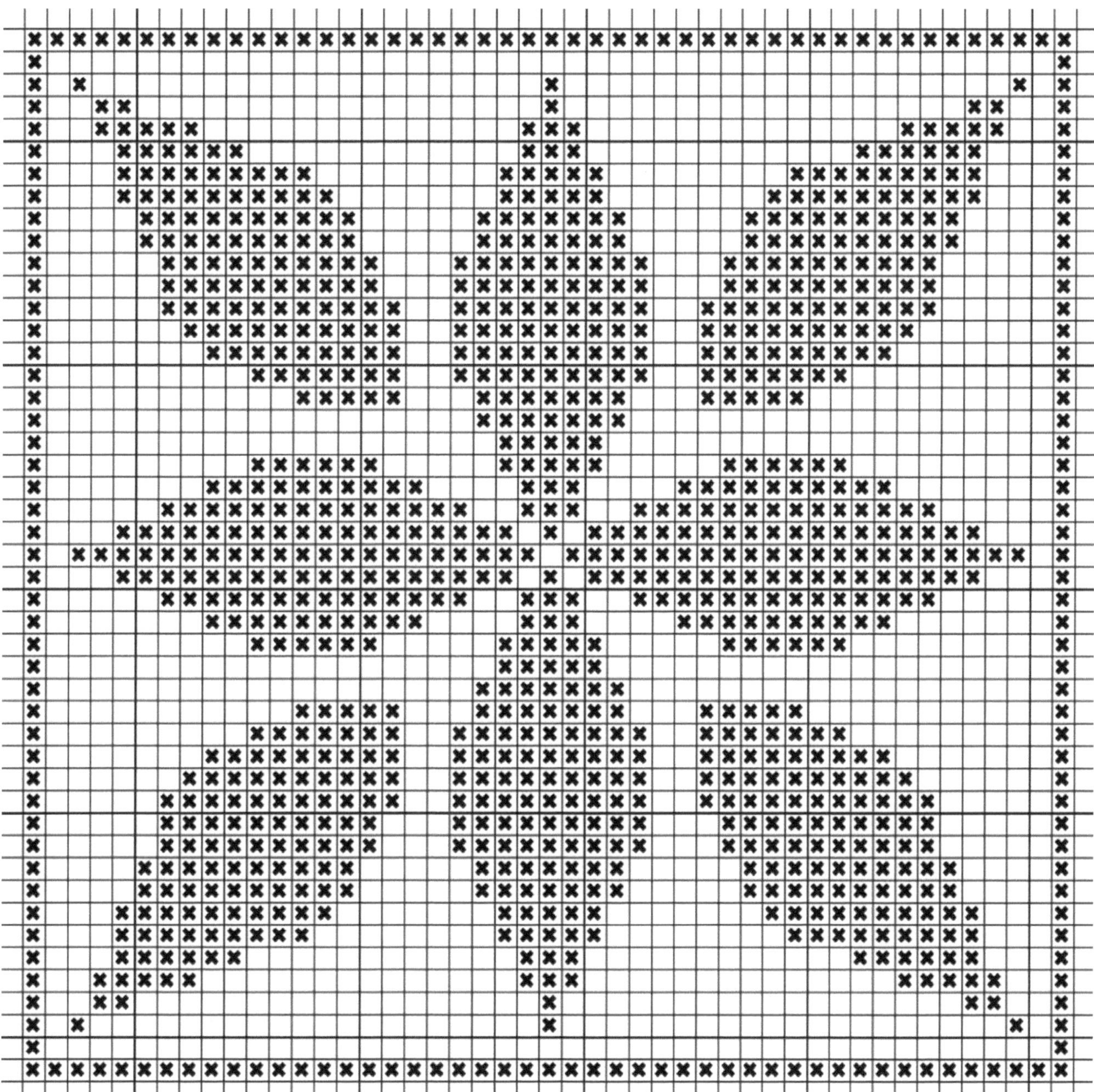

INDIVIDUAL BLOCKS – 2

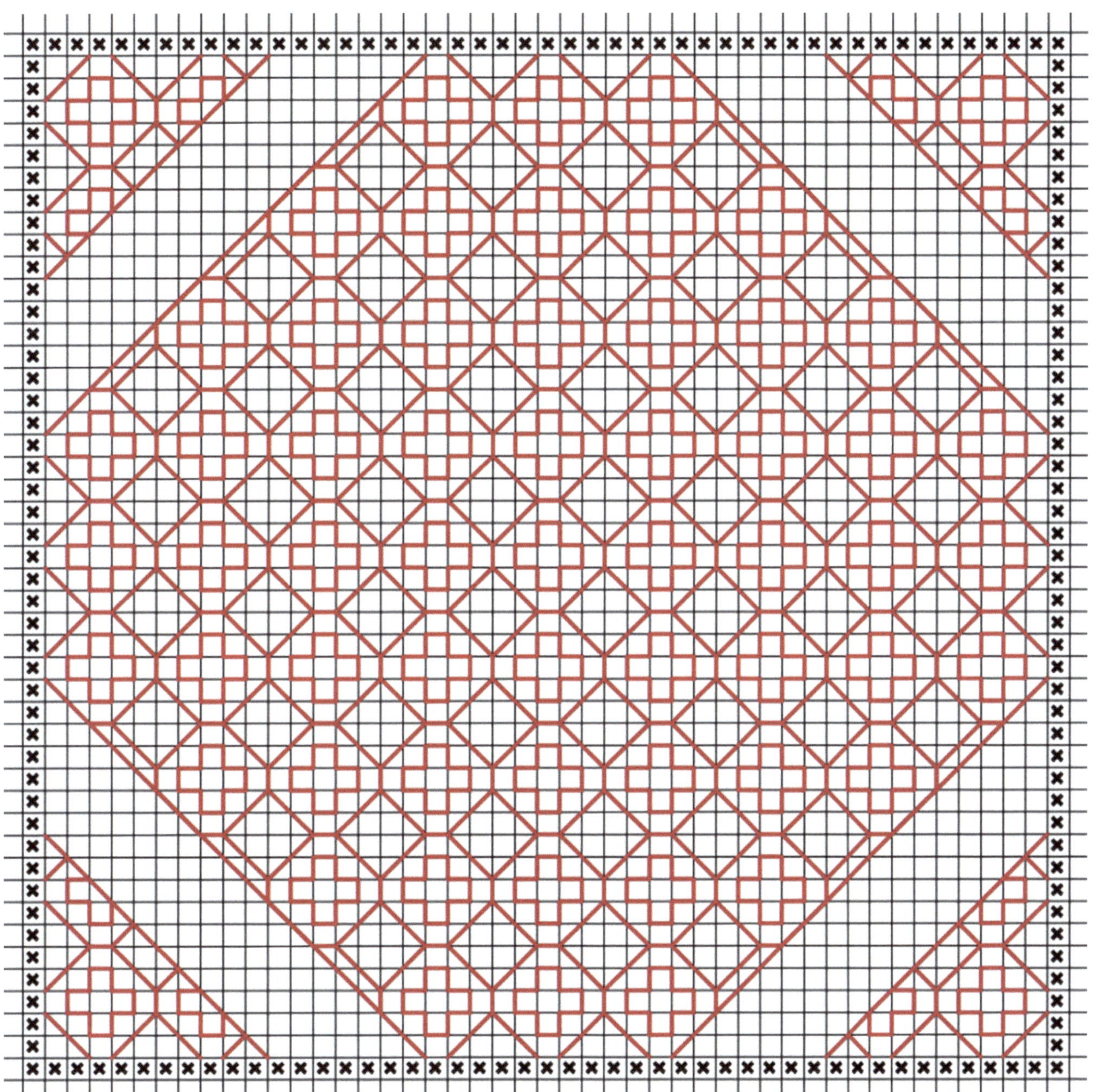

INDIVIDUAL BLOCKS – 3

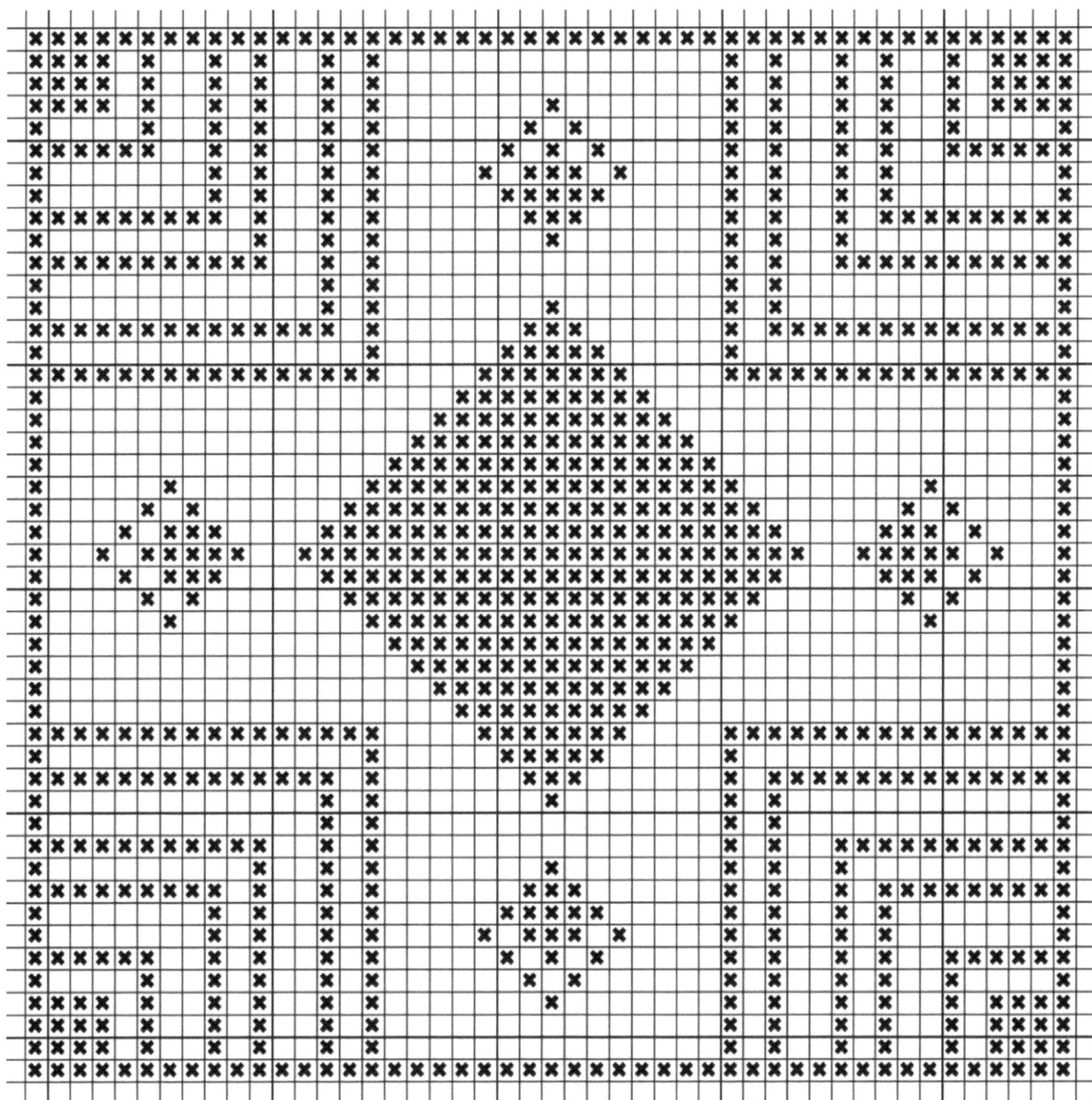

INDIVIDUAL BLOCKS – 4

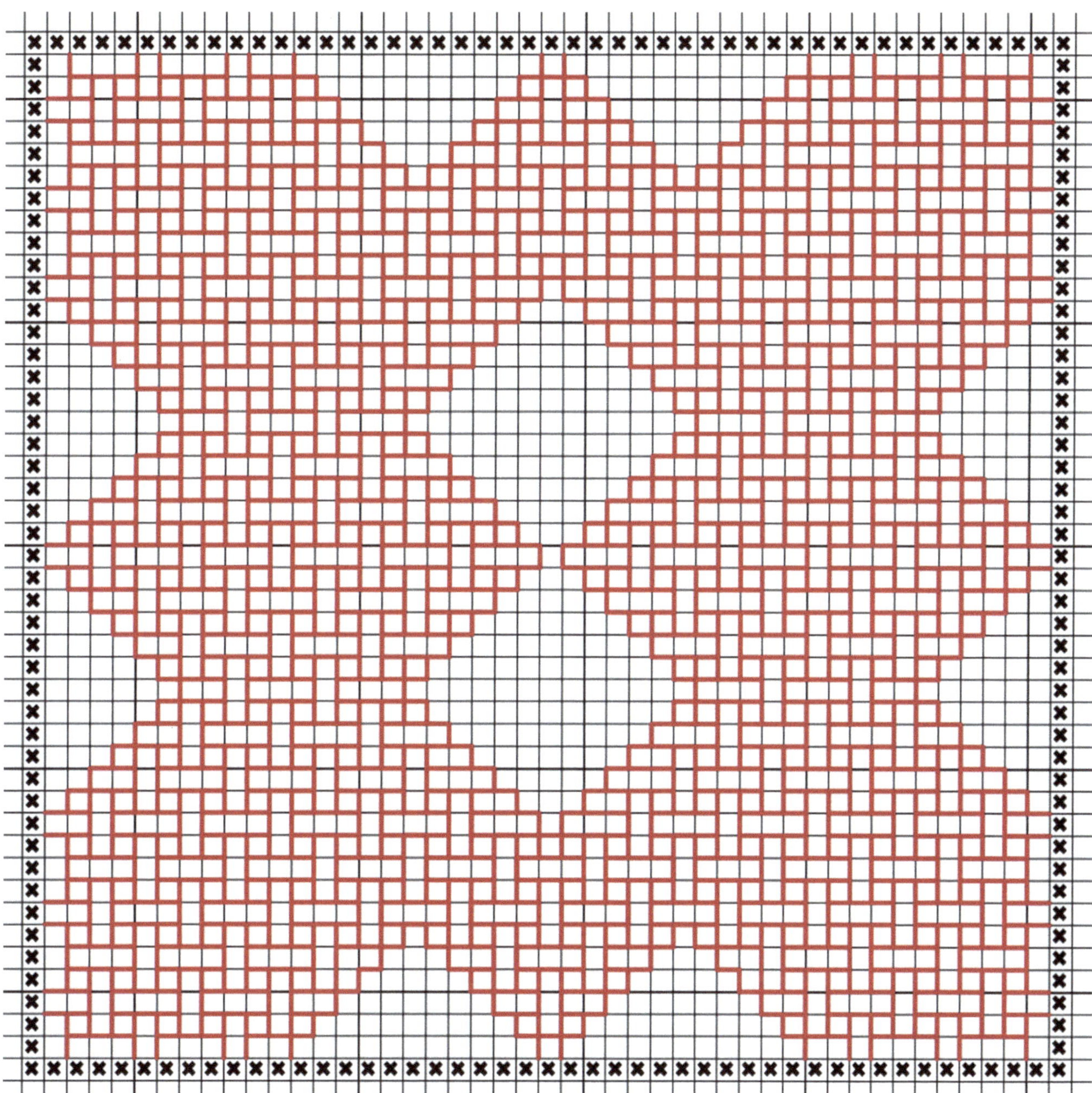

INDIVIDUAL BLOCKS – 5

INDIVIDUAL BLOCKS – 6

INDIVIDUAL BLOCKS – 7

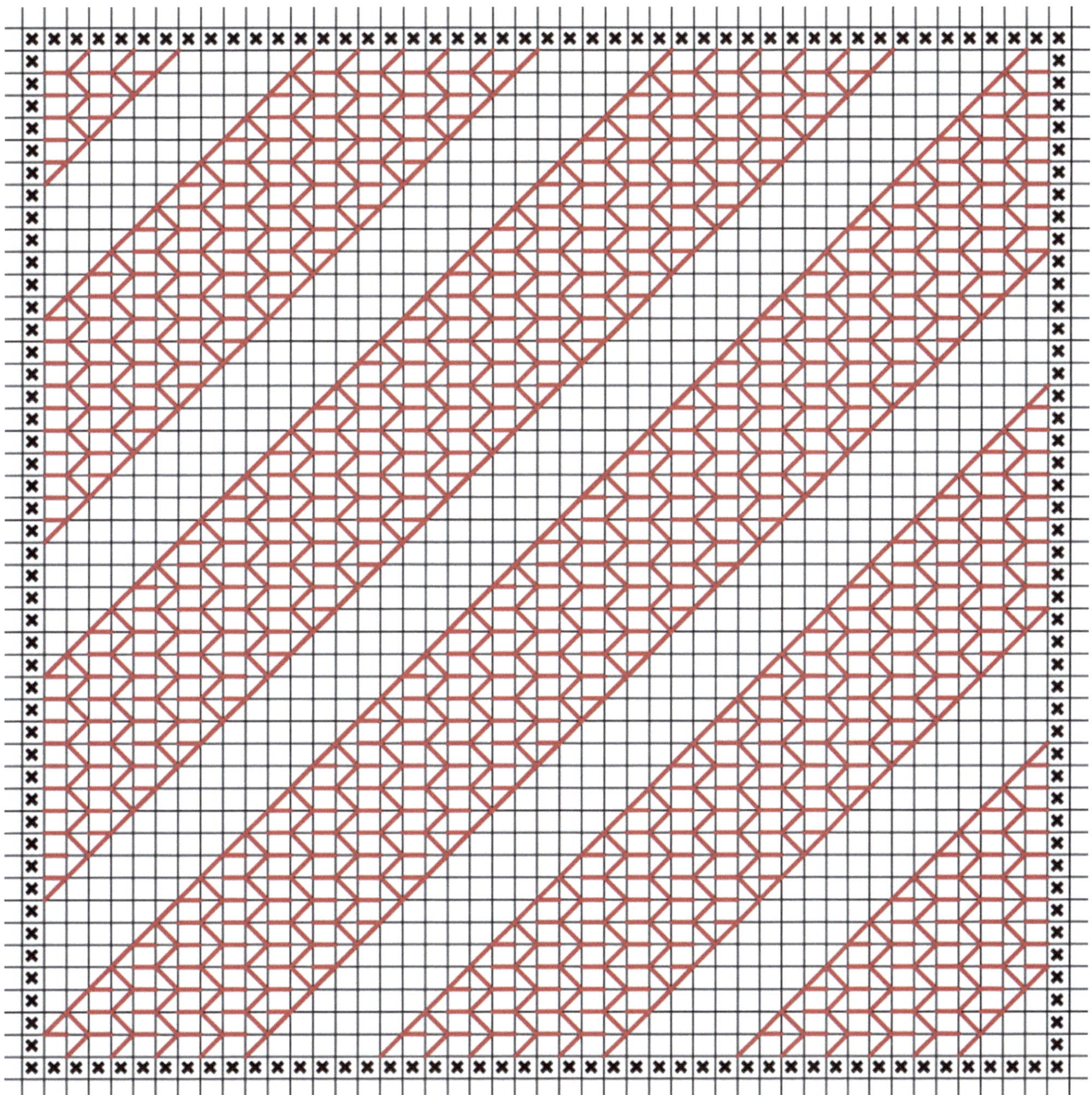

INDIVIDUAL BLOCKS – 8

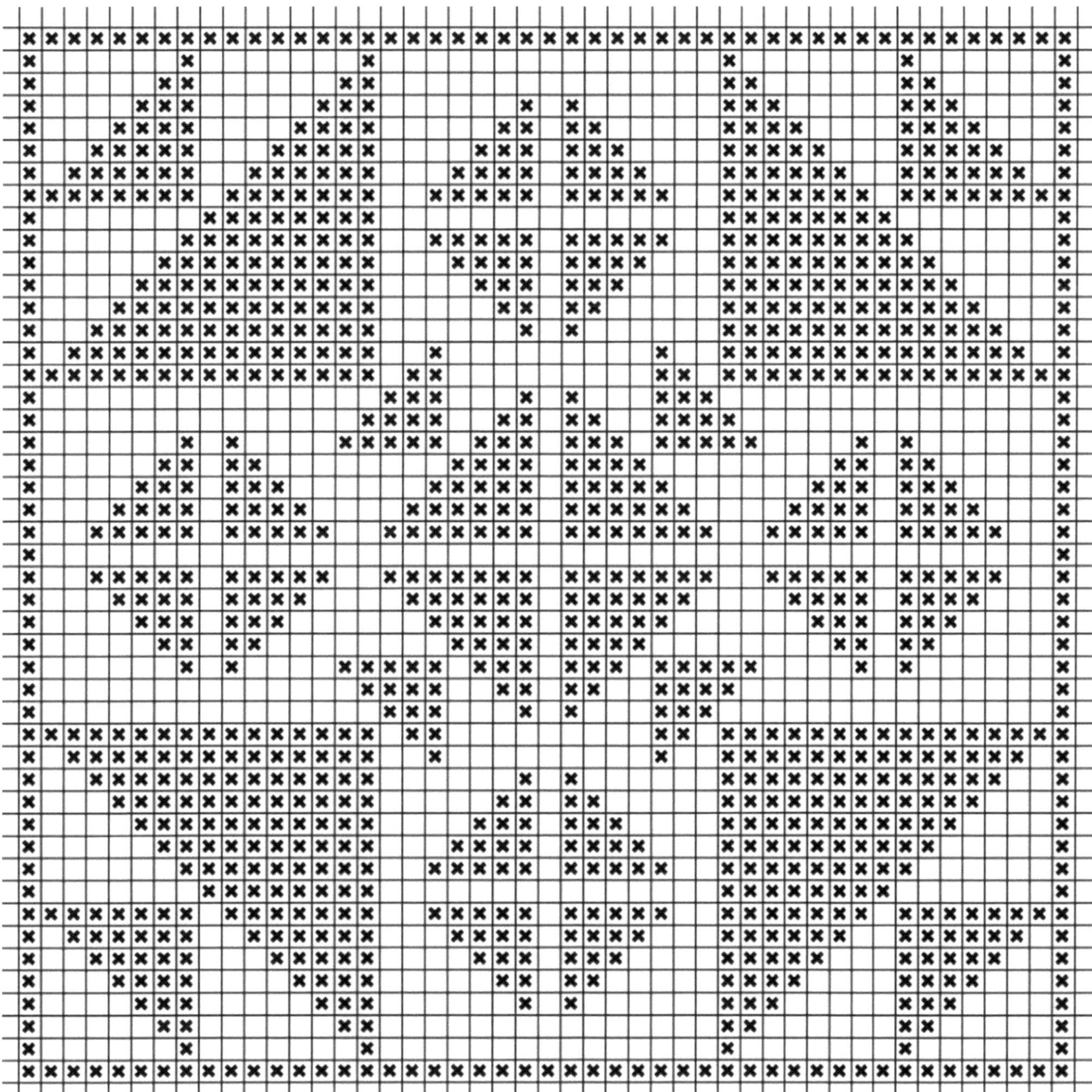

INDIVIDUAL BLOCKS – 9

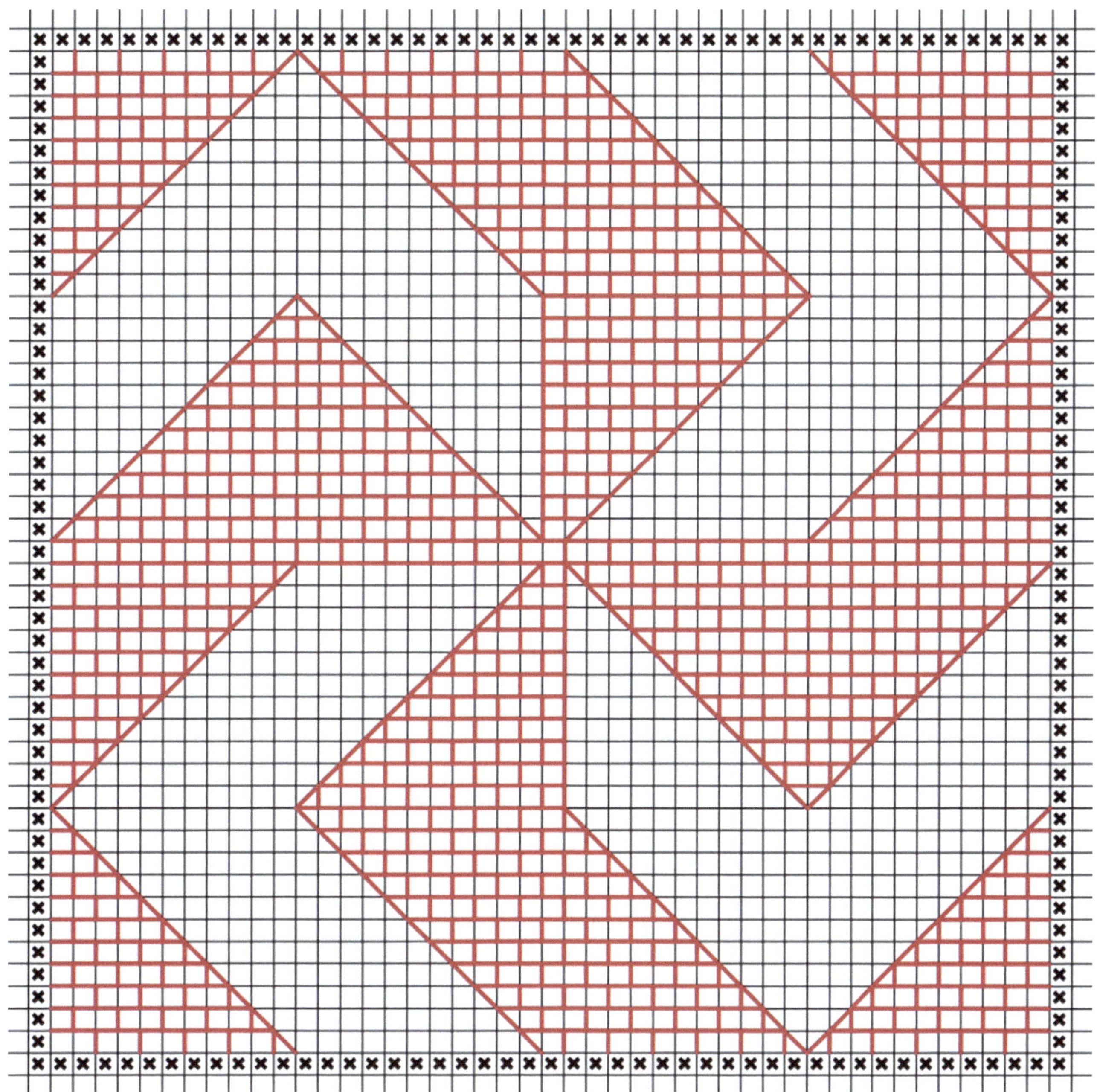

INDIVIDUAL BLOCKS – 10

INDIVIDUAL BLOCKS – 11

INDIVIDUAL BLOCKS – 12

ABOUT THE AUTHOR

Loretta Oliver has been publishing cross stitch patterns and information at StitchingtheNightAway.com since 2001 with a goal of sharing the joy of cross stitching with others worldwide.

Her first cross stitch project was when she was 8-years-old and a love of the fiber arts was born, she's been stitching ever since. In the online world she found a vast community of amazing stitchers and creative people to share the love of needlework with and found that connecting with those people made her love the hobby even more.

Eventually growing a website and community, creating her own designs, helping others learn to stitch and encouraging people to explore new stitching techniques, fun fibers, different design styles, and more.

Find out more and connect with Loretta at www.**StitchingtheNightAway**.com

Stitching the Night Away is a cross stitching and needlework website where Loretta shares her designs, offers free patterns, plus tutorials, tips, resources and tools for crafty stitching folks. Be sure to check out the Fabric Calculator app and sign up for the newsletter while you're there.

www.ingramcontent.com/pod-product-compliance
Lightning Source LLC
Chambersburg PA
CBHW042002110726
48006CB00004B/966